MY JOURNEY FROM PARIS TO JAVA

T0124628

First English Edition of Honoré de Balzac's *Voyage de Paris à Java*

ENGLISH TRANSLATION © Barry Winkleman 2010
DESIGN AND TYPOGRAPHY © Editions Didier Millet 2010

CONSULTANT: Associate Professor John N Miksic

EDITORS: Timothy Auger, Ibrahim Tahir
COVER DESIGNER: Pascal Chan
DESIGNER: Lisa Damayanti
PRODUCTION MANAGER: Sin Kam Cheong

First Published in 2010 by
Editions Didier Millet Pte Ltd
121, Telok Ayer Street, #03-01
Singapore 068590
www.edmbooks.com

Printed by Mainland Press, Singapore

All rights reserved. No part of this publication may be reproduced, stored in a retrieval system, or transmitted in any form or by any means, electronic, electrostatic, magnetic tape, mechanical, photocopying, recording or otherwise, without prior written permission from the publisher.

ISBN 978-981-4260-14-5

HONORÉ DE

BALZAC

MY JOURNEY FROM PARIS TO JAVA

Translated by Barry Winkleman

Made according to the methods taught by Charles Nodier in his book *Histoire du roi de Bohême et de ses sept châteaux* [History of the King of Bohemia and his Seven Castles] in the chapter that deals with the various means of transport in use with certain authors, ancient and modern

edm EDITIONS DIDIER MILLET

Contents

Foreword — 7
Nigel Barley

Preface — 11
Pierre Janin

My Journey From Paris to Java — 17
Honoré de Balzac

Afterword — 55
Jacques Dumarçay

Bibliography — 64

Foreword

An important myth of European history sees the Age of Discovery as a time when the world was dramatically stripped of false enchantment, when it was measured, assessed, mapped and objectively known by Westerners for the first time. Accounts of the first official expeditions to China have all the overburden of raw data that accompanies a contemporary moon shot and such knowledge – it is said – brought economic expansion, scientific truth and the global exchange of information that created the modern world of our everyday experience.

Yet, an alternative history can be written, whereby the West took its ideas with it as it travelled, transforming and projecting them onto the world that it found, so that many of the new places visited were not so much 'discovered' as merely fixed on the map, since they had been invented in European thought long – sometimes centuries – before. California, the land of Prester John and Patagonia were all 'known' as mythical places long before they were geophysically located and Columbus died still doggedly convinced that he had reached distant India. What actually developed in the wake of such voyages of discovery was a literature rich in fantasy and metaphor in which authors freely copied from each other, exaggerated and invented, for the boundaries of the possible had yet to be set in stone and the world was still a place of infinite possibilities where women could conceive simply by being exposed to the heat of the sun and the coconut was really a dragon's egg waiting to hatch. The pages of these works swarm with a lavish bestiary of strange creatures, bizarre cultural practices, absurd products of Nature and it is impossible to predict in advance which would turn out to be 'true' and which wholly phantasmagorical. Thus, although Stamford Raffles, that most sober of natural historians, would be careful to qualify exaggerated reports of the deadly qualities of the Javanese *upas* tree – whose exhalations were said to cause birds to drop dead from the sky above it – his description of the devil's beetle box (*Rafflesia arnoldi*) with its stench of rotten flesh and carnivorous diet, seems no less improbable but just happens to be accurate.

The intoxicating and romantic possibilities of the exotic would be deliberately embraced in the 19th century, and cultivated and playfully fashioned into escapist fantasies of armchair travel. Balzac's *My Journey from Paris to Java* clearly belongs to this genre and deserves to be more widely known as a classic. Yet its sensuous women, political animals and visions of incalculable wealth and extraordinary luxury, all have their parallels in allegedly factual works of much the same date. Indeed, such phantoms have never been banished from our imaginations and dreams. Every high street travel agent is a solid testimony to their enduring power and Balzac would have been the first to understand that, in the age of satellite navigation, we still orient ourselves by such mythical maps that alone have the power to nourish and console us.

Nigel Barley

Preface

It would be fair to bet that on picking up this book and seeing its title, more than one reader will exclaim in amazement: "I never knew Balzac had been to Java!"

On this point there can be no doubt, as all his biographers agree that Honoré de Balzac never travelled to the Far East.

Our author suggests as much himself on his last page: "if it were possible to have been in Java more truly than I, who had not been..." This remark is made at the end of the book and it is true that after enjoying its fables and fantasies, the reader will already have become aware that this was the case, without necessarily being an expert on Balzac or on Java.

The book's genesis can be found in the meeting between the 30-year-old Balzac and an honorary Commissioner of Ordnance, Monsieur Grand-Besançon, at the home of some friends in the town of Angoulême.

In 1831 the young novelist was no longer unknown. *The Physiology of Marriage* and *The Chouans* had both been published successfully a year earlier. But nonetheless, just before undertaking his *Human Comedy*, Balzac found himself fascinated by Grand-Besançon's evocative tales of his oriental travels. Sensing that his audience was hooked, Grand-Besançon had no hesitation in embellishing his memories of his marvellous travels. When Balzac talks of a reincarnation of Sinbad the Sailor we would be tempted to see an anticipation of *Tartarin*[1].

Thus it was that, the half-mocking, half-credulous Balzac decided to write his fantasy, *Voyage de Paris à Java*, and published it in the *Revue de Paris* on 23 November 1832, having spent much time correcting and making additions to the proofs.

The story is written in the first person and would seem to indicate that the narrator is Balzac himself. In fact, at the very end, Balzac wrong-foots us. He claims to be just the narrator's interlocutor and that the narrator is in fact M. Grand-Besançon, who is identified by his initials.

A certain embarrassment is evident in this retrospective attribution of the story to someone else. Balzac knew that this high fantasy was not really his style. In addition, a quick enquiry had convinced him that Grand-Besançon had made up quite a lot. Thus, just to take one well-known example, the

---

1 Boastful fictional hero of French novelist Alphonse Daudet.

book describes the fearful *upas*, the poisonous tree that can kill instantly anyone who inhales its vapours. Unfortunately, ten years earlier, a genuine explorer, one Dumont d'Urville, had exposed the whole story as a myth in his book *Voyage Pittoresque autour du Monde* ("A Picturesque Journey Round the World"). "Among these trees, there is one that has featured in the most absurd stories, the *pohen upas*, or poison tree. [...] These fairy tales now make naturalists smile...".

Here, then, is a journey to Java recounted by someone who has never been there and who has himself been told many stories that are just that – what are, in every sense of the word, stories. Had his purpose not been so clearly of a different order, Balzac's reputation as a realist would have suffered. And let us take note of what the title page says: the book is "made according to the methods of Charles Nodier[2]...", to whit, as an armchair traveller.

Romanticism, dominant in this period, preferred the vast, dreamy world of the imagination to the harsh, industrial realities of the day. Besides, the references to Robinson Crusoe and Sinbad the Sailor clearly place the book alongside imaginary voyages rather than with more scientific accounts.

The protestations of authenticity that appear throughout

2 Charles Nodier (1780–1844), French writer and member of L'Académie française (French Academy).

are quite normal in this kind of work. It is thanks to its element of fantasy that it provides such a magnificent view of Balzac's imagination. In the pages of *Voyage de Paris à Java*, the young novelist's entire dream world of the East is revealed.

Every period has its own Orient: for the 18th-century Enlightenment China was considered the epitome of wise, philosophical government that we should take as a model. (One can see that Balzac was not the first to let himself be fooled thus.) For this Orient of the Age of Reason, romanticism substituted another that was quite the opposite: made up of wild passions, despotism, cruelty and also love – where nature was stronger and more extreme than elsewhere, that's to say Europe.

For Balzac, Java was all Orients in one, from India to Indo-China. What better territory than an island to serve as a distillation of the "soul of Asia" to which Balzac refers in his conclusion? Insularity is the epitome of a closed, finite world, of a universe in miniature where the image of the entire Orient can be found. To European eyes everything is overblown on this exotic island: feelings are stronger and purer, passions more dangerous but by the same token more authentic and more exalted. European society in contrast seems insipid. "In Paris you live as you please… and boredom soon sets in. But in Java, death is in the air."

Paris and Java – two civilizations that the story sets in opposition to each other at every turn. Presented with the women of Java, the Bengal sparrow, the flower of the Volcameria tree – we are to sense, implicitly or not, a comparison with a Europe in which "our books, our poets, our women, everything – are all just small." Beyond the fables of Java, Balzac turns his pitiless gaze on European society and in this ironic and shifting vision the real Balzac appears, the one who shouts at the reader, interrupting his narrative to deliver judgements and thoughts – in sum, the great Balzac.

Published at the very dawn of Balzac's great period, *Voyage de Paris à Java* is nonetheless considered a secondary work. Certainly, some passages stretch one's credulity and appear irrelevant. Nevertheless Balzac loved this book and often referred to it later in his career. The Javanese woman certainly lent some of her sensuality to Paquita Valdès in *History of the Thirteen*. Again, a note on the rarity of Macassar oil certainly evokes *César Birotteau*. Specialists have found an echo of this fabulous Orient in many of Balzac's books. What counts is that this minor work supplied the oriental references of the great Balzac – it forms a library of dreams. There could be a worse fate.

Pierre Janin

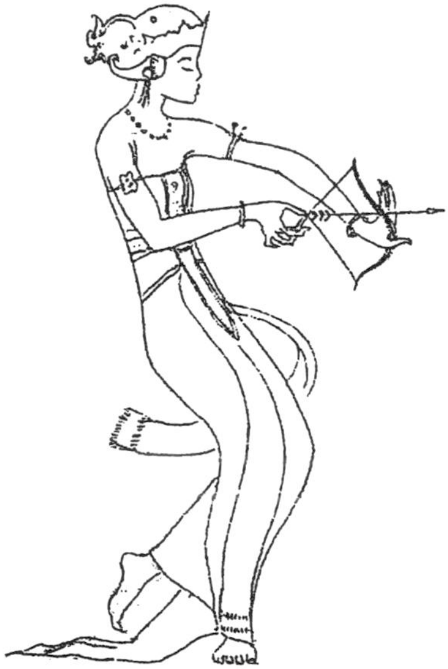

My Journey From Paris to Java

For many years, like the late Robinson Crusoe, I had been tortured by the irresistible desire to go on a long journey. Day by day the Ganges peninsula and its islands, the countries of the Sunda Strait and Asiatic poetry in particular became the objects of my obsessive hopes and desires. Is an obsession a good or a bad thing? I do not know. To some we owe new political systems or great works of literature, others lead straight to the madhouse. Nonetheless, while waiting for an answer to this difficult problem let us just note the high cost, in everyday terms, of ideas such as these.

Travel to the East Indies is very expensive and while it is easy to calculate one's expenses while making the journey, it is impossible to contain them if one does not actually go – they then become quite ruinous. How many hours wasted, not to mention the damages caused by absent-mindedness – a hot poker falling on the carpet, an upturned inkpot, a burnt slipper – supposing you to be an artist, a writer, a man of imagination.

No. Just count the precious moments crazily lost in hours daydreaming in front of marbled arabesques on the chimney breast. Now, time is money; even more, it's pleasure. It is the immeasurable quantity of things conceived in its abyss into which all things go and from which all things come and which devours and creates everything. Doesn't daydreaming amount to the same thing as stealing from your delightful mistress, or from yourself, so happy with her? To show how much I have wasted, sometimes one word in a sentence, a newspaper headline, the title of a book, names such as Mysore or Hindustan, my spilt tea leaves, the Chinese scenes painted on my saucer, a mere nothing would fatally set me off through a maze of daydreams, on a fantastical ship, and on my imaginary journey cause a thousand delights to spring up before me.

Among my most expensive possessions are two Mexican vases sold me by Shölcher that cost me three or four hours every day ... as I put down the book in which I was looking up some vitally important information, coming across words such as *Bayadère*, *Colibri*, *Sandal*, *Lotus*[1] – griffins that carry me off to a world of scents, women, birds and flowers. Then I catch sight of a fleeting chimera on one of the Mexican vases that shows a rabbit in an armchair lecturing a snake that's sporting a moustache and wearing spurs – symbol of a thousand bits of literary or political tomfoolery. Then, plunged into a pointless meditation of the sort that's forbidden fruit for manual labourers and writers, two similar groups, I continue to inhale Indian perfumes. I lose myself in these splendid lands to which England is now restoring their old magic. The imperial luxury

1 Indian dancer, humming bird, sandalwood and lotus.

of Calcutta, the wonders of China, the island of Ceylon, that island so favoured by the Arab story-tellers of old and Sinbad the Sailor – overwhelm all the charms of Paris.

Finally, I go from dream to dream and end up doing nothing, and being completely captivated by a kind of nostalgia for an unknown land.

One day in November of 1831 in the heart of one of those beautiful valleys in Touraine where I had gone to be cured of my oriental obsession and on a delightful evening when our sky had the purity of an Italian sky, as happy as a chaffinch, from Méré manor, where Tristan had once lived, I was brought to a sudden halt in front of the old castle of Valesne by the ghost of the river Ganges which stood before me. The waters of the Indre metamorphosed into those of that vast Indian river. I mistook an old willow for a crocodile and the massive stone walls of Saché for the svelte and elegant buildings of Asia. It was incipient lunacy so to misrepresent the beauties of my own country. It was time to put things in order. Everything had been said. I decided to leave, despite the harshness of the weather, on my journey through the possessions of their Dutch and British Majesties. With the impetuousness typical of a man from Chinon, I went at once to Tours, boarded the stagecoach and drove off to pick up some commissions from two friends who lived en route. I wanted to embark at Bordeaux, trusting in the famous saying: all roads lead to Rome!

No words can express my happiness and calm as I drove along in the coach that was of course taking me to Chandernagor and the Laccadive islands. As I knew for certain that I had now started my long journey, Sumatra, Bombay, the Ganges, China, Java and Bantam left me in peace as I now contemplated the monotonous fields of Poitou with an indescribable pleasure. I was saying my farewells to France. At every village I asked myself:

"When will I see it again?"

There was in my determination a sort of eccentricity, as Lord Byron would have called it if he were still alive, which set me apart from any ordinary traveller. I was going to set off in the clothes I was wearing, with six shirts, a couple of razors and some light bags, as if I were just calling in on a neighbour. I was taking no anti-cholera pills, no blunderbuss, no tent, no camp bed, none of the thousand useless things that travellers take with them. I understood perfectly well that wherever you live, the business of living should be the same everywhere and that the fewer rags I took the better off I'd be.

To justify to myself this enforced destitution and to turn it into an act of stoicism, I recalled the profound philosopher, who, during the last century, had walked round the world, apart from some sea crossings, entirely on foot, without spending more than fifty Louis per annum. Frederick II of Prussia wanted to meet him and arranged a parade to this end. The traveller, who was French, refused to ride a horse, so the King let him stand in the middle of the square in Potsdam. He ordered his troops to treat the man as an obstacle and the cavalry opened their ranks for him. Frederick asked him if he could do anything for him and the pilgrim begged the King to enable him to draw in Berlin the money that had been reserved for him in Dresden. This stroke recalls that sublime response of Diogenes to Alexander the Great – "get out of my sun" – on a similar occasion. My aim was to imitate this Frenchman, now forgotten, whose great knowledge and economic flair were so admired by Frederick. I have never been able to discover the fate of this walking Lapeyrouse.[2] I can spend hours pondering the drama of his fate – so rich, but so little known. How many men, laden with treasures of knowledge as he was, have perished on deserted strands with the world of science none the wiser?

Also, in order to be useful to my neighbours at the Observatoire Royal, I thought I should take great pains on my travels. Had I not reported back the correction of an error in the best known of latitudes or in the obscurest of longitudes; had I not collected the tiniest of unknown molluscs or revealed some fault in the zero meridian – all scientific researches to which I am, by the way, completely alien, I would have looked upon my journey as being the equal, in such riches, of the tales of Lords McCartney[3] and Amherst,[4] or any such Lord you want among the explorers of Africa, Asia and Australia etc., who have always struck me as being utter charlatans. I promised myself that my account of my travels would be coloured by fantasy so that it could be read equally well by scientists as by children, and believed by those who will believe anything incredible.

I arrived in this state of mind at Angoulême, which I wanted to make my base. Well, before going any further I went to the explosives factory build by General Rutty on the banks of the Charente River. This factory, conceived in monumental style, cost the state a mere million – and the government, naturally, manufactures almost no gunpowder in it at all, due to our passion for contradiction. It's a truly French characteristic which is seen everywhere. Thus, have you seen in Paris a placard outside a shop advertising waterproof boots

2 Baron de La Peyrouse (1744–1818), French botanist.
3 British Ambassador to China (1737–1806).
4 British Governor-General of India (1773–1857).

or hats? You can be sure that they will let in more water than others. Let us be fair to our government – it perfectly matches our lack of substance and our Gallic spirit. From this point of view it is eminently typical of the nation. Between the starting point and the conclusion of our revolutions, not forgetting the placards of our shopkeepers, we must admit that in France we always end up in precisely the opposite place to where we wanted to get to when we started.

But since a parliamentary investigation into administrative blunders was not the aim of my journey, this government factory won my admiration; and, not feeling any desire to be critical, I found myself, the following evening, after recovering from my exhaustion with a good night's sleep, seated round a joyful fire with three friends.

With your permission I will eschew the foolish personal stories with which my predecessors have started their tales. To get to the point, project yourselves at once across the ocean and the Asian seas, traverse the great spaces on a good sailing brig, and let us come at once to Java, my island of choice. If you like it, if my observations are of interest, you will have been spared all the boredom of the journey.

Nonetheless, if you're like me, I pity you. I confess, to my shame, the things that beguile me the most in such tales are precisely those that I understand the least.

When a traveller talks to me of emerging from I don't know which islands, of monsoons, currents, the number of fathoms of water found at a place which I worry about as if they were the bones of Adam, of reefs, records, lochs, high and low gallants, boat tackle, of bolt ropes, sideslips, the state of the sky etc., of flowers and plants ending in –*ia*, of the class of dicotyledons or dichotomons, orobranchoids, with fingers, etc., or of nudibranchs [a kind of mollusc], or clavipalped tentacles, globular horns, marsupials, hymenoptera, dipteroids, bi-valves, no-valves (how do they manage?) etc. – then I open my eyes wide and try to grasp something out of this deluge of barbaric words. Like people who stop on the Pont-Neuf to look down to the river at nothing in particular, seeing everyone else doing the same thing – I am searching for the unknown in the void with all the passion of the chemist seeking to make diamonds by compressing carbonised wood. Such books fascinate me in the same way as staring into an abyss. Reading an incomprehensible work such as *The Apocalypse* – and there are many apocalyptic books in modern literature, above all accounts of scientific travels – is like a game of skittles in the darkness for my soul, like Jacob's struggle with the angel of the Lord. And often it is no more permitted for me to see the angel than it was for the patriarch.

"Java! Java! Land! Land!"

Back to our subject.

I swear that for a European, above all for a poet, no country is as delicious as the island of Java. I will talk about the things that imprinted themselves most vividly on my mind, in no particular order, but as my memory dictates. What travellers forget is mostly unimportant anyway. If I fail in literary terms to be strictly logical, I will be so in the order of my impressions. Thus I will concentrate first on the most immediate and personal matter for a man disembarking from a ship.

In Paris you live as you wish: playing, loving, drinking as you please – and boredom with it all sets in very fast. But in Java, death is in the air. It hovers round you in the smile of a woman, in a glance, in a fascinating gesture, in the undulations of a dress. There, if you have the conceit to want to fall in love and to indulge your weaknesses – you will quickly perish. How many pernicious seductions are born of that enforced good behaviour! Do not succumb to them, you must keep a strong hold of yourself, stay sober above all, keep your spirits up with reviving waters and do not go off and waste your energy. Then, having written your *Mane*, *Tekel*, *Phares*[5] on your tablets you will find yourself in the presence of the women of Java. Becoming virtuous on pain of death, you will find yourself faced at every step with the vexatious temptations of St Anthony, less his pig.

First, accept as a principle that Javanese women are mad about European men. Next, let me describe for you the admirable species of the fair sex that lives in Java. Women there are as white and smooth as the finest vellum; no shade of colour touches their complexion; their lips are pale; their ears and their nostrils – all are white; only their fine black eyebrows and their brown eyes contrast with this bizarre pallor. Their hair is wonderfully luxuriant and just by shaking it they can seem hidden under a pavilion impenetrable to the most ardent gaze – and this veil falls to the ground on all sides. This precious ornament, of which they are unbelievably proud, is the object of the most meticulous care. These beauties of the island use up the entire production of Macassar oil that the East Indies produces. So when it was explained to me that no more than a couple of litres had ever found their way to France, I could not think, without laughing, of the fortune M. Naquet made from selling little bottles of the stuff in the thousands. If you had ever run your hands through the abundant and scented hair of a Javanese lady you would feel nothing but contempt

5 The words Daniel saw at Belshazzar's feast, in the Bible.

for the pathetic bit of stubble that European women hide so easily under a bonnet.

Most of the women are rich and, many of them, widows. Soon after arriving, a European can make a marriage as rich as any he dreamt of during his long, cold nights back home. The unbridled luxury, the seeking of the unknown, the poetry of the languid life of Asia combine with the seductiveness of Javanese women to lead you into a fatal folly – above all after a long sea-crossing.

There, all eyes burn with the languid beauty of a gazelle, there, white bejewelled feet, that I have always called fairy's feet in the manner of Perrault, lie on silk and cashmere cushions.

A Javanese woman of distinction only ever wears a muslin blouse, which hangs from the neck to the floor and is tied round the waist by a simply coloured silk belt. Her diamonds and pearls, the rings and jewels are strewn among the slaves who serve her. If palm and betel nuts darken her teeth at least her breath is always sweet.

It is rare for a European to resist the sight of this fairyland. As for me, I succumbed, in spite of the fearful warning written on the foreheads of these ladies who have almost all been married five or six times and have been widowed five or six times. What is there more tempting for an artist than a struggle with these pale, frail, delicate vampires?

During the long periods of melancholy and secret despair that I lived through for twenty or so years, I more than once nearly succumbed to the sweet pleasures of suicide without ever having ventured further than the edges of the moat surrounding the Bastille, at the time when it was empty of water: but the most delicious of my planned suicides was to die from a surfeit of love. I can think of nothing more poetic or more gracious than the sweet langours, the moments of utter prostration which would have certainly led me to oblivion. Well! I found the fulfilment of these crazed dreams in the typical Javanese marriage. It is love in all its poetry: passionate love, unrequited love, love without remorse. Javanese women never weep over the man they bury – having worshipped him more than God, they just forget all about him. There's a similarity here to the perfection of some machine that crushes its inventor. Elsewhere, you live for love – in Java it kills you. Heartless love then seeks its next victim just as Mother Nature herself follows her own sweet way and takes no notice whatever of her own creatures. Thus Javanese women consume many European men.

Maybe we should pack off some husbands to Java just as the English send over shiploads of young English girls to Bengal. It is quite extraordinary that nobody in Paris has thought of proposing this outlet to lieutenants bored with the military, to poets without fame, to actors without roles and to all those likely to go to Sainte-Pelagie prison. It's a more natural branch of commerce than conscription and the press gang known as *remplacements militaires*. Blasé people should all go to Java – they would find life as vividly coloured as the *Death of Sardanapolis*. You live on top of a bonfire!

I was saved from my sweet torment by an accident. My Javanese lady died and I really missed her. Before I left for the Ganges she made me the most romantic of Javanese gifts – a lock of her hair pasted on to a card. When I show this incredibly long strand of hair to people as a curiosity, a lot of them are incredulous and think it's something quite different. And there are days when even I no longer believe in that hair myself – but they are days when life is empty for me.

A local scientist has offered me proofs, which are not without merit, that the whiteness of Javanese women is due to the singular way they grow their hair. I will keep these documentary proofs for scientists as well as some other details that should not be made public and which may throw some light on certain physiological matters.

Nevertheless, before passing to other issues it is important that I counter one point crucial to the reputation of Javanese women.

Since my return I have read some pieces about the Javanese travels of a very distinguished naturalist, who only got to relax when he was in Surabaya, where he stayed only a short time. He described Javanese women as being, on the whole, quite ugly. If he were talking about Malay women of the lower or middle classes I would agree with him. The pale Javanese women with that luxuriant hair whose customs I have described are rich. Besides, in every country there are huge differences between women of the aristocracy and those of the lower orders.

The same author insisted specifically that the fair sex in Java was inclined to be very jealous. He attributes the sudden deaths of many European men to the revenge of Javanese women, who, he says, are highly accomplished in the preparation of certain poisoned beverages. Although the women of this island scarcely need this accessory to kill their lovers or husbands, whom they speedily devour, I willingly believe in their jealousy and its sinister effects. There, where love is so deadly, so rare, every woman must guard her treasure like a miser.

I admit that the secretiveness of Javanese women and their silent acts of vengeance are unlike any among European women. I had noticed their richly coloured characters and at first had thought them better than they are, but I do find on the other hand that they have a poetic quality and a beauty that is enriched by these two other passions. They want you so completely that they will not forgive you even one glance at a rival. But if the pleasures of their company are so dearly bought and so perilous it must be recognised that they are also immense. Just as poetry, painting and science are all-consuming for scientists, painters and poets, these women are just as jealous and implacable as genius. Their love is a real fire, it burns.

The day after my wedding, by poetical chance, which increased the delirium of the sweetest of awakenings, I heard for the first time the song of the Bengal sparrow.

If the island of Java were one day to lose the wonderful finery of its eternal spring, its beautiful sites, its virgin forests, its shimmering city swarming with every race on earth, where the luxury of the Indies melds with the luxury of the west, if it were to be deprived of its voluptuous houris, if the sparrow were all that was left, it would still be vital to make the pilgrimage to Java to appreciate to what degree nature surpasses man in musical science.

I cannot put into words the sensations aroused by the Bengal sparrow of Java. Its music is all-embracing. Its song, like some rich memory, implies every poetic possibility. Sometimes its voice evokes the new and delicious impressions of first love. Sometimes it speaks of one's fatherland and childhood and sometimes it echoes the fantastic and indescribable dreams of the most spiritual melancholy. Then suddenly it will create with grace and without effort the long-sought-after effects, the difficulties overcome, that are the glory of the virtuoso – the pearly cascade of the piano, the tenderness of strings, the warm sounds of the *physharmonica*. It is the cantor of real passion.

Listening to the Bengal sparrow when only your soul has preserved its potency alongside a satisfied Javanese lady, is one of those indescribable Asian pleasures. The bird speaks your thoughts once more, sings of the silent sensuality in your eyes, expresses the pleasure that has just left you and gives it a second life thanks to the aphrodisiac grace of its music. It speaks to the heart, which it arouses just when the senses are still. Perhaps this sparrow is a soul in ecstasy.

Prodigal nature has decked it out in gold, purple and emeralds – diamonds and jewels fly around you. But this poor little flower of the air loses its voice beyond the Azores. This divine bird lives on the nectar of roses and is nourished by their scent. It is faithful in love. It is a rose among roses in Bengal and Java, with which it is so madly in love that it can only exist in a rose's calyx. As soon as it sees a rose it flies to it, stretches out in it, bathes in it, rolls in it. It kisses it, sucks it, tramples it and sings its gentle trills to it. It seems it finds another life in the rose, the one to which we all aspire. Perhaps no human passion can compare to that of the Bengal sparrow for its favourite rose.

Unluckily I have a perverse ignorance of everything relating to natural history, so that I am reduced among all its marvels to making simple observations. I can therefore not tell you how many feather remiges this avian poet possesses, nor at which precise point its nostril pierces its beak, nor if its mandibles are in good shape, nor in what state are its tarsi. Besides, this bird is mine! It belongs to me for only I have understood it. This bird, or its music at least, is a secret between my soul and the sky just as the melancholic poetry of certain of Weber's phrases is a mystery shared only by two lovers.

Understand this – I am one of your egotistical travellers,

a species forgotten by Sterne in his classified list of travellers. I have never claimed to research the nature of the terrain nor to issue reports on *Flora javanica.* I have just let myself go with the flow of my imagination. It has been as an amateur and a poet that I have seen what I have seen. It is perfectly possible that I have judged Javanese women in the manner of the Englishman who judged the women of Blois after only one sample. So if I lie, it is with the best will in the world.

Nevertheless there are things that one cannot doubt even if when back at the family hearth, the events of our journey take on, to our own eyes, fabulous colours embellished by the poetry of memory or by the emphases of the narrative which assume a lyrical colouring and the most ordinary of incidents take on the charm of the personal story of he who can say: *I was there and this happened to me.*

So, having described for you the Javanese woman and her murderous passions, and the marvellous voice of the Bengal sparrow, whose song is a book of beauty, I am forced by my memory to speak of the volcameria tree whose flower is to the sense of smell what the Javanese woman is to passion and the Bengal sparrow is to the ear: the same mental phenomena in the soul of a man who is enough of an artist to breathe in the reviving perfumes of these divine corollas. The crowns that Indian women put in their hair are braided with tufts of volcameria. They certainly recognise its immense power.

The scent of the volcameria enters your being humbly, with the diffidence of that of violets. Then it invades you, turns into a taste, becomes full of sap on the palate and reminds you confusingly of the delicacy of a strawberry, the spicy savour of the pineapple, the viscous pleasure of a cantaloupe melon, but all beautifully blended with the ethereal quality of a pure memory. This occult creature persists, it invades the mind, pierces and shakes it like jasmine from the Azores, or some distant tuberose. It is a thousand scents together, all delicate, all fine and elegant and above all fresh; they cavort in the soul like dreams, they tickle and wake the maddest and most cheerful ideas. You return to the flower like the Bengal sparrow to its rose, you inhale it with deep breaths without wearying. Its scented breezes never tire you in their inexhaustible variety. There is something feminine in the sighs of its flowers. You would say it was a tender mistress at whose side you were chatting, voluptuously, of an evening. Humid scents! Despairing creations! But what a beautiful creation – its fabric is thick and velvety like a camellia, its colours gentle as the apricot tree. Its flower is composed of fifteen or twenty tiny roses with rounded petals arranged like one of those rose windows that our architects copied from nature to decorate our temples. These little roses, dark at the edge and almost white at the centre, are lovingly squashed and form a domed tuft like a hortensia. This flower and its exquisite perfumes belong essentially to people who adore music, who are hungry for romance and who are devoted to prayer.

To listen to the cry of the Bengal sparrow, inhale the scent of the volcameria, or pass your exhausted hand through the hair of a woman of Java, in the open under a red sky in the humid atmosphere that the Chinese know how to arrange when they lay out their long, damp rice-straw mats in front of the windows of your quiet, silk-clad and cashmere-draped palace … ahh! This life is a spiritual and poetic indulgence which cannot be expressed in any ecstasy. For those who have enjoyed it there are no arts, no music, no masterpieces. Yes, Raphael's Madonnas, the harmonies of Rossini, the orchestra of the Bouffons, the efforts of the French perfume industry, our books, our poets, our women – all shrink in comparison. Europe is impotent: God and Asia alone have been able to create such pleasures as words cannot describe – like the mystical hymn of two hearts locked in their vivid embrace.

Finally, in this island of miracles, all is harmony, everything sets life ablaze, devours it and you return a dead man. Only one sense remains to be seduced there – and that is satisfied in a manner appropriate to the most uncontrollable of desires. There, taste spurns the fruits of Asia in favour of an admirable nutrient. I mean tea: the tea that is picked in the lands near China. Its narcotic effects make it for me an agent of pleasure to be ranked between opium and coffee.

Wine, coffee, tea and opium are the four great stimulants that immediately act on the brain by the impulse they give to the stomach and that compromise substantially the ethereal nature of the soul.

Let us leave wine to the poor. Its vulgar drunkenness disturbs the organism, without giving much pleasure in payment for the damage it does to the body. Taken moderately, however, this liquid imagination can have some effects that are not without charm. One must no more vilify wine that speak ill of one's neighbour. For my part I do owe it some recognition. Just once in my life I tasted the joys of this most ordinary of gods.

Do allow me this digression: it may remind you of a comparable moment in your life.

Well then, one day I was dining alone with no temptations to hand other than a bottle of wine whose bouquet was incisive and full of volcanic odours – I have no idea on which stony slope it had ripened, but I forgot the laws of temperance. Even

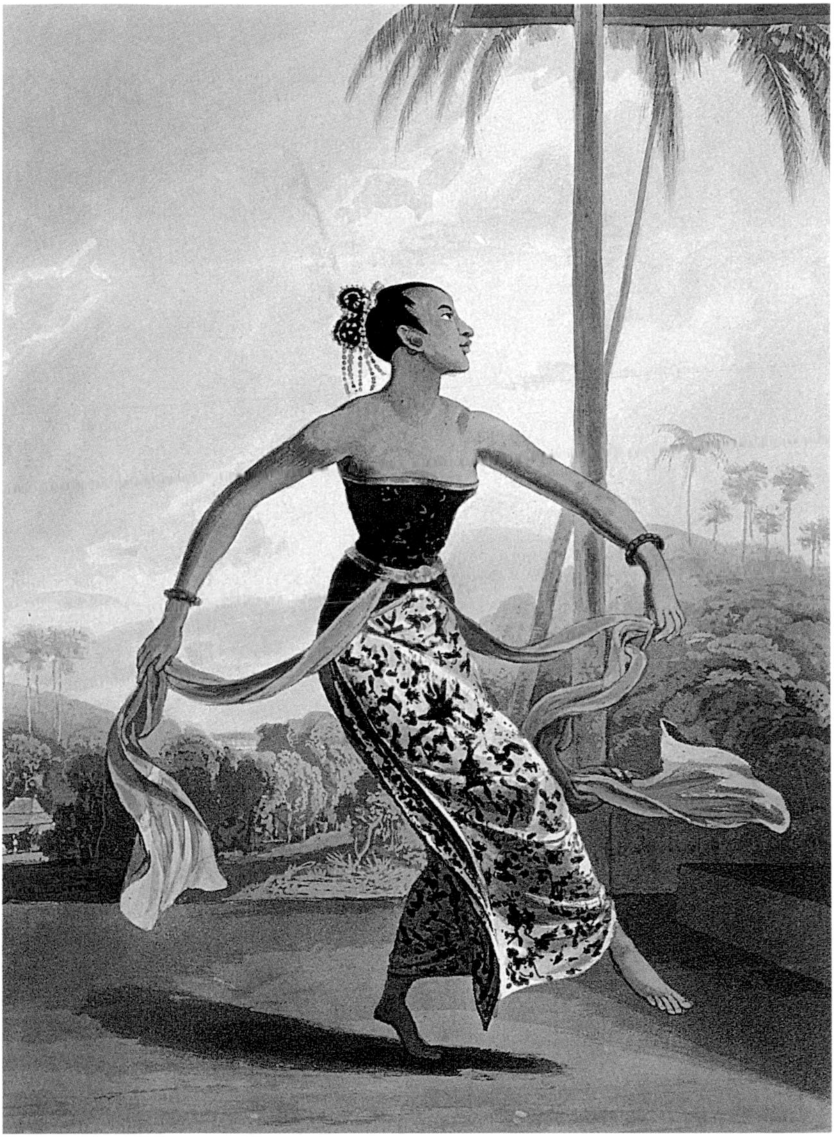

… the female genius has developed further than anywhere else on the globe …

L'ARBRE UPAS.

(Arbre upas à l'ile de Java.)

... the upas grows at the centre of an extinct volcano, whose awful miasmas it exhales and where, by the caprice of nature, it pumps out appallingly harmful substances ...

33 Tom. VII. N° 24

Premiere CEREMONIE NUPTIALE, *des* PEUPLES *de* JAVA. *Le* MARIÉ *va chercher la* MARIÉE.

Seconde CEREMONIE NUPTIALE *des* PEUPLES *de* JAVA, *le* MARIÉ *conduit la* MARIÉE *chez lui.*

… soon after arriving, a European can make a marriage as rich as any he dreamt of during his long, cold nights back home …

… what is there more tempting for an artist than a struggle with these pale, frail, delicate vampires?

... that the whiteness of Javanese women is due to the singular way they grow their hair ...

... it is rare for a European to resist the sight of this fairyland. As for me, I succumbed, in spite of the fearful warning written on the foreheads of these ladies ...

… in this island of miracles, all is harmony, everything sets life ablaze, devours it and you return a dead man …

… all eyes burn with the languid beauty of a gazelle …

so I went out standing reasonably upright, but I was solemn and silent and found astonishing vagueness in the humanity and earthly circumstances that surrounded me.

On the stroke of eight I took my seat in the circle at the opera, almost doubting that I was actually there and not daring to admit that I was in Paris in the middle of a dazzling society, whose faces and dress I could not distinguish. Delightful memory … while I felt neither pain nor joy, a sort of happiness dulled my pores but did not enter my inner being. My soul was drunk. What I heard of the overture to the *Thieving Magpie* resembled those fantastic sounds that fall from the skies into the ear of a woman in ecstasy. The musical phrases, stripped of the imperfections men put in their works, and bursting with everything the artist had of the divine, reached me through brilliant clouds. The orchestra seemed to me like a vast instrument where some kind of work was being done but whose movement and mechanics I could not grasp, able to make out but dimly the shafts of the double basses, the scraping of bows, the trombones' golden curves, clarinets and lights – but no men, only one or two powdered immobile heads, and two swollen grimacing faces … I was nodding off …

"This gentleman smells of wine," said the low voice of a woman whose hat brushed my cheek, or whose hat I, quite unaware, was brushing with my cheek.

I confess, I was annoyed.

"No, Madame," I replied, "I smell of music."

Then I left, holding myself remarkably straight, but calm and cool, like a man snubbed who leaves his critics with the vague sense that they have chased away someone of superior gifts. To show this lady that I was incapable of drinking too much and that my smell must have been an accident and quite foreign to my habits, I thought I would get myself over to the box occupied by Madame la Duchesse de … (let's keep her name secret) whose fine head was framed so remarkably in feathers and lace. I was irresistibly drawn to her by my wish to ascertain whether this unbelievable *coiffure* was real or due to some fantastical optical illusion with which I had been endowed for the past few hours.

When I am there, I thought, between this elegant woman and her affected and prudish friend, no one will suspect me of being three sheets to the wind and they will remark that I must be a man of importance.

But I was still wandering through the endless corridors of the Theâtre Italien without being able to find the damned door of this box, when, the show having finished, the crowd rushed out and pinned me to the wall.

That evening was certainly one of the most poetic of my life. At no period had I seen so many feathers and so much lace, so many pretty women, so many of those little oval binoculars with which the inquisitive (and lovers) can examine the contents of other boxes. Never have I shown such energy, nor such character – which, were it not for the self-respect that I owe to myself, I would call obstinacy.

The tenacity of King William of Holland in the Belgian question[6] is nothing in comparison to my perseverance in standing on the tips of my toes and maintaining a pleasant smile.

However I suffered outbursts of anger, and sometimes wept, and this weakness places me well below the King of Holland. Then I was tortured by awful thoughts, thinking

6 See Afterword.

of what that lady would rightfully think of me if I were not to reappear between the Duchess and her friend. But I comforted myself with contempt for the whole human race. Nevertheless, I was wrong. That evening at the theatre there was good company and everyone took good care of me and took the trouble to let me pass.

Finally a very pretty lady offered me her arm as we were leaving. I owed this courtesy to the high regard in which I was held by Rossini, who said many flattering things to me, which I quite forget but which must have been supremely witty – his conversation is quite the equal of his music.

This woman was, I believe, a Duchess – or maybe an attendant. My memory is so confused that I believe in the attendant rather than the Duchess. Nevertheless, she wore feathers and lace… Always feathers! Always lace!

In short, I found myself in my carriage. It was raining torrents but I don't remember being touched by a single drop of rain. For the first time in my life I tasted one of the most vivid and unpredictable pleasures in the world, an indescribable ecstasy – crossing Paris at eleven thirty at night, rushing past the street lamps, seeing the multitude of shops pass by, all the lights, the signs, the people's faces, groups, women under umbrellas, street corners fantastically lit up, dark squares; observing a thousand things through the rain that one had the impression, wrongly, of having seen somewhere in daylight. And still feathers, and still lace! Even in the pastry shops.

Certainly, wine is a powerful force!

As for coffee, it causes a most desirable fever! It enters the brain like a Bacchante. When it attacks, the imagination runs around, dishevelled, stripped naked, twisting around like a python and in this inspirational paroxysm a poet's abilities are multiplied a hundredfold. But it is intoxication of the mind, as wine intoxicates the body.

Opium absorbs all human strengths, concentrates them, strengthens them to the power of two or three, raises them to a degree of potency I cannot guess, and gives to the whole being a sense of having been created in a great void. It gives to each sense its greatest sum of voluptuousness, irritability, fatigue, exhaustion: opium is a death desired.

But between opium, which is so treasured by orientals, above all by the Javanese who buy it at ten times its weight in gold; between wine and coffee, whose abuse is entertained even in Paris, nature has placed tea.

Tea is taken in large doses in countries such as Java, where the leaf is still fresh and has lost none of its precious aromas. With tea are poured all the treasures of melancholy, dreams, evening escapades and even the ideas inspired by coffee and the voluptuousness of opium. But caprices snatched from the brain are played out in a grey and vaporous atmosphere. Its ideas are gentle and you are not deprived of any of the benefits of a healthy body: the state you are in is not sleep but rather the indistinct somnolence of early morning daydreams.

In Java you find tea already made, to hand in every shop. You enter and you can drink one, two, three cups helping yourself from porcelain bowls and there is no need for polite thanks. You behave as you would in Paris when lighting your pipe at the gas lamps outside tobacconists.

All these pleasures together – the Javanese women, the flowers, the birds, the perfumes, the daylight, the air, this poetry that puts so much soul into each of your senses make me say, since my return from the East Indies:

"Happy are they who go to die in Java!"

In fact, life's problem is not its length but its quality, the number of sensations it affords. Well, in this admirable land, always green, always varied, a meeting-place for all nations, eternal bazaar, where pleasure grows of itself, where the greatest freedom reigns, where there is room for all superstitions – there emotions, pleasures and dangers abound in a way that makes your very core vibrate. And this is why the Orient boasts so few writers. One lives too much in oneself to have anything left of the self to hand out to others. What is the point of thought, there, where all is feeling?

I wasn't long in Java before hearing about the local marvel – the *upas*, the only tree of its type in the world and whose awful effects cast so great an influence over Javanese customs. According to the island's traditions, the *upas* grows at the centre of an extinct volcano, whose awful miasmas it exhales and where, by the caprice of nature, it pumps out appallingly harmful substances which it is distilling continuously. Tofana, Brinvilliers,[7] the science of chemistry, indeed humanity in all its capacity for evil-doing, is surpassed by one tree, by one of its leaves even, and by a pure chance of nature. It is enough to dip the point of a dagger into the bark of the *upas* tree, with one quick cut, to lend the blade the properties of cyanide. As soon as this toxic steel pricks the skin of a man, he drops dead at once with no convulsions or any sign of pain. Not only does the sap give the steel this power of death but the tree exhales its murderous vapour so quickly and with such intensity that its shade will kill a man who stays under it any longer than is necessary to prick the trunk with his dagger. In any case this operation can only take place windward of

7 Two notorious French poisoners.

the tree. Air, as it passes by the tree becomes fatal in the immediate vicinity. If the wind changes during the short time a Javanese spends staining the point of his dagger, he expires at once.

Animals and birds and all living things recognise this dreadful effect and fear it as a throne of death. Offshoots of the main tree grow all around and form a fearful enclosure through which few people pass. This sinister plant grows in solitude. It reigns there, an image of those ancient Asian kings whose look could kill.

You will understand that naturalists confine themselves to conjecture about this unique tree, not directly observed; and as it allows no strollers or artists anywhere near, it has escaped the attention of our all-powerful magazines. But since science is not usually wrong, scientists have bravely classified it as one of the species of *Strychnos*, trusting in the received wisdom of the Javanese.

The following story illustrates the philanthropic means by which the natives get hold of this insidious poison. When a Javanese is condemned to death by his tribal leader he will be pardoned if he can successfully bring back a poisoned dagger. No more than three or four out of ten criminals escape the caprices of the *upas* tree.

I obviously wanted to see this singular tree and I approached it from the windward side at a prudent distance. Armed with a telescope I could tremble quite at ease at the frontier of this kingdom of terror, to which Danton and Robespierre should have been transported. I cannot remember ever having seen in my mind's eye, either in the mass graves of the Bible, or in the most fantastical scenes of a corpse-strewn literature, a spectacle of such appalling majesty.

Imagine a field of whitened bones, an enclosure worthy of the *upas* tree, a testimony to its power, victims here and there, thinking themselves saved, piled up round the tree. Their skeletons, struck by the sun of the Indies, gave off sharp rays of light, reflecting the sun. The play of light among the remains had horrific effects. There were heads whose eyes still shone, skulls that seemed to curse the sun, and teeth still biting. These are the only human corpses that are not food for worms … thrown into this circus that has athletes but no spectators, the most awful silence broken by the cracking of bones – is there a worse sight in all the world?

The Javanese are as proud of their *upas* as the people of Bourges are of their cathedral. And I will not hurry to refute the rather sketchy information hitherto provided on the *upas*, in deference to the honest natives who took me to see this monumental tree.

Despite the claims of many travellers it is certain that there is no rival to the great Javanese *upas*. It is a jealous ruler that it would be difficult to dethrone. It is the only individual of its species to have reached that height. I thought it was between ninety and a hundred feet high. Its offshoots are as big as our five-year-old saplings.

It is the case that Javanese and Europeans wanting to clear a part of the forest fear coming across an *upas*, but until now, even if some trees of this species, even the *Strychnos*, have been encountered, they have proved quite harmless and to exhale the poison necessitated substantial chemical procedures. A *kriss*, the Malay dagger, dipped in any other poison, causes a slower death that is preceded by convulsions. And then, when the *kriss* has served its purpose, if the owner wishes to restore its venomous powers, he can revive it with lemon juice. Now I would like other travellers whose imaginations may be less slothful than mine to verify these facts that have a great historical importance for science, which I can only authenticate as an eye-witness without a scientific reputation and whose chimerical memories are not notably reliable.

And again, the difficulty of getting this terrible poison can be proved by one fact. The Malays place an enormous value on their *kriss* and never sell them. On this island the *kriss* has the same value for a Malay that a good mare has for an Arab. This poisoned dagger is the entire fortune of a Javanese. Thus armed, men pay no more attention to a tiger than we do to a cat.

On my return from the district where the *upas* grows I lost a lot of my fear of tigers, having seen the ease with which the Javanese get rid of them. The tiger is the most cowardly of creatures. It finds it hard to attack a man even when it's hungry. If it misses its strike when it leaps at him it will never try again but just slopes off like a clumsy footpad. When men who have been condemned to death refuse the *upas* tree option, they are normally made to fight a tiger that has been kept starving in a cage, armed only with a lead-bladed dagger.

When the condemned man is from a rich or powerful family, the justice minister substitutes a steel blade for the lead one, which is most unconstitutional, but there is an aristocracy everywhere, even among savages.

This combat, of immemorial antiquity and a clownish and cruel act of justice, offers the natives a spectacle of which they are very fond. I must admit that this execution is infinitely more amusing than the extremely monotonous drama we put on in the Place de Grève.[8] At least the subject has a chance and if he wins at least society has not lost a man of courage. The spectators form a circle with the effect of an enclosure. The condemned man, whether he has the good or bad dagger, almost always has to go and provoke the tiger to force it to leave its cage and fight. With the iron dagger the Javanese always wins, but with the lead one the outcome can be undecided for a long time.

Javanese men are brave, hospitable, generous and good. Even so, opium can sometimes send a man into a fury and in his stupor he often vows to kill everyone he meets. This vow is called *amok*. This frenzied tendency is so well known that when a Javanese runs through the streets with *amok* in his head, the locals come out of their homes without too much fear and go to meet the madman, holding in front of them a long pitchfork with which they grab him by the neck; others just throw a noose round his neck and strangle him there and then without ceremony. To be sure, this custom could be dangerous in Europe. Plenty of people could be said to run *amok* without being aware of it. But since our civilisation has not taken that path, our pitchforks and nooses could not be used even to kill off a rich uncle, for example. This incontrovertible fact – and it annoys me to say it – proves that our customs lack elegance. There is no wit in our society, which is just a market for good and evil.

When I returned from my excursion to the interior to view the *upas* tree I noticed remarkable flowers that were like no others known to me. But, ignorant of the ways of the herbarium, I just stuck them in the pockets of my waistcoat. The result was a great loss for collectors, and even more so for

8 Parisian place of execution.

me, since I muffed the chance to see my name, elongated by an *–ia*, in all the learned dictionaries and among horticultural classifications. Nevertheless I saw a vegetable growth of such magnificence in the midst of all the trees, one that was in such sharp contrast to their massive forms, that it is engraved in my memory like an antediluvian leaf preserved in a block of gypsum. But can any traveller ever really describe to his listener the impressions he has received, in all the varieties of beauty with which nature has momentarily dressed them? Our most valuable treasures are those rare memories that we retain here and there from life whose intimacy and eloquence cannot be described by human speech and for which there is no word and no poetry – the word and the poetry for these things are hidden deep within us.

At the moment when two happy beings say sweet words to one another there is an effect of sunlight, as it suddenly falls from the sky upon a mass of green, such that it seems to pour onto the landscape all the magic qualities of a feeling that seems just too vast for feeble hearts. Then nature shines on with both its real charms and with those conferred by human illusion. For these dazzled eyes to which all is happiness, the fantastic shape of an old willow and its beautiful leaves becomes an indelible image because the soul has endowed it with its exuberant powers and has embraced it with that inexplicable passion which moves us to grab and smash an exterior object in those moments when joy has so increased our strength.

During one of these supreme moments under a cloudless sky on top of a rock that extended, like a promontory, into a wide expanse of sapphire-blue water, I saw, like palm trees offering the hope of an oasis, that sublime plant that I must call a tree-fern.

Imagine one of our European ferns whose stems are fine and supple like those of a young poplar, growing to a height of a hundred feet. Add, layer upon layer of pairs of enormous leaves, so mobile, gracious and delicately worked, like coloured watermarks, incomparable in their variety; and send rays of light through their serrated diamond-shaped leaves. Try to see through this verdant lace the shining waters of the lake. Then contrast the aerial marvel of this wonderful plant resembling the final flourish of a firework display with the imposing solid mass of an Indian forest with its huge leaves and pullulating vegetation … and finally, see a twisting road hugging the lake like a giant anaconda coiled on the sand. Now imagine yourself in a palanquin carried by silent slaves and now try to imagine one sweet trembling hand saying to another hand: *I love you.*

Then, all of a sudden the tree fern appears at a sudden turn in the path like the living poem of eternal love. Ah! It's *The Song of Songs*, sung silently – the immense picture of an immense happiness, a monument made for this festival of the heart like those that peoples make for their religious festivals. Is not a religion the heart of a people?

The tree fern would not have appeared to me in such an exceptional way had not the circumstances made it unforgettable. It is, I was told, an annual, one of these botanical rockets that take off and die in the East Indies with such grace and incomparable sparkle.

I was busier looking at the monkeys, to my shame, rather than at the *Flora javanica.* I wanted to study the habits of these animals, who are so close to us in the great chain of being whose end and whose beginning are unknown to us. Thus was I initiated into a few Javanese superstitions.

On this island, every animal species has its own high priest who knows all about his flock in great detail. This high priest is always some old Malay whose family has inherited all the traditions that from time immemorial have accrued on the customs and habits of the animals in their apostolic care.

When I expressed the wish to pay a visit to the monkeys, my dear Javanese lady took me to see their pontiff, telling me that he would teach me about the curious characteristics of the great family of which he was the guardian. We betook ourselves to a Javanese village belonging to some tribe or other whose *tomogon* – the title given in this country to the chieftain of any population group – was known to my guide. We found the monkey father seated at the door of his hut on a sort of settee made of bamboo. It is bizarre but perhaps natural to man to imitate the gestures, accents, manners, attitudes and words of his friends, and this old Javanese bore a marked resemblance to a monkey. His face was triangular and hollow, his deep-set eyes without brows had a certain brusque vivacity and his movements had the rapid precision characteristic of the noble dynasty of monkeys.

My beautiful companion, without getting down from our litter that had been carried by her barefoot slaves with admirable speed and preceded by one of their number who cleared away the snakes, had explained my wishes to Toango, the name of this venerable ecclesiastic, and he came up to us at a sign from his *tomagon*. There was then an exchange of questions and answers between the two Indians and my lady.

My astonishment was great, when Lady Wallis (my Javanese lady was the widow of an English sea captain), translated the answers of the monkeys' cardinal.

It was impossible to accede to my wishes today, she said, becausc the monkeys of some tribe or other had, for several months, been battling another group of monkeys who were trying to seize a part of the forest whose wildlife and produce belonged to the first group, and it would be dangerous for a European to get into the middle of the fight.

I was keen to question the old Malay and she served as my interpreter. I learnt that the monkeys who lived under the protection of Toango were divided into tribes. Each tribe comprised a certain number of monkeys of the same species, and obeyed a chief who was constitutionally elected. They instinctively chose as *tomagon* the most skilful among them just as tartar horses choose as their leader the most beautiful, swift and strong horse. Each tribe owned a limited amount of the forest. Frequently, as with men, one tribe invaded another and the quarrel was settled by a battle in which all the monkeys of each tribe participated without any need of military conscription and other inventions belonging to monkeys of a higher intelligence.

Toango could not tell me how the monkeys were able to designate in advance the place and time of the combat but their rites of war demanded that assignations were respected in good faith. The females trotted up and down at the rear and carried off the dead and wounded. If the attackers were victorious they merged with the vanquished tribe; if not they retreated to within their borders.

Toango told me all about the depravity of their customs. Lady Wallis listened to him with the utmost seriousness without blushing even when he proved, with examples, that we humans were sadly not alone in our debauches. He confirmed to me the curious fact of the abduction of a young Malay woman by a Javanese orang-utan which had kept her for a very long time and fed her with all the care of a lover. English newspapers had told the strange story of a similar event at the Cape of Good Hope. Then, having spent time with Toango and his people, we returned home.

On the way to see the old Malay I had noticed a big herd of buffalo watched over by a child in a sort of prairie at the bottom of a valley crowned by woods that rose in tiers as in an amphitheatre.

When we passed by for the first time this child was busy mixing a coat of earth and dung that he painted on the buffalos which indulgently allowed him to cover them with it. I expressed my astonishment at seeing animals being groomed in a way so harmful to their health; but Lady Wallis told me that this coat was a necessary protection against the stings of a gadfly that were so venomous that it was not unusual to see these animals die from the seizures that resulted when these insects fastened on to them. The thick layer with which their little keeper dressed them protected them totally from the attacks of their enemies.

"Nothing can describe," she told me "the friendship that these great brutes have for this little child … he can lie down and sleep among these animals with nothing to fear. If they fight or become enraged not one of them would hurt the child. Males, females, young ones would jump over him without touching him; but if one of them hurt him, even by accident, the others would gore the guilty one to death."

Just as we were passing this place again I had the pleasure of witnessing a curious scene that proved the truth and strength of this singular affection. The buffalo were standing in a circle forming a horned girdle, their eyes like carbuncles and shining like torches. All, moved by the same thought, had run to surround the child … a tiger had leapt from the wood to come and devour their little guardian. But although the ravenous beast had leapt with the speed of an artillery shell, before it could get to the sleeping child the buffalo had already formed their circle, and one of them caught the tiger with his horn and tossed it ten feet in the air and at once all the others trampled it to death underfoot. This was one of the finest spectacles I have seen. The buffalo, having executed their victim with the judicial *sang-froid* that is their hallmark, started grazing peacefully again. So sure was he of them, that when he awoke their innocent guardian showed not the slightest fear nor uttered the smallest cry.

On the day chosen by Toango I came back to his house armed with a good supply of rice, a meal and all the accessories. Then we headed off to the forest where the monkeys lived. When we had reached a clearing doubtless well known to the old Malay, he spoke a word to my slaves who laid the table and served dinner.

Toango had brought along a sort of tom-tom to summon his citizens and he deafened us with his discordant music and with the strange cries that he uttered.

At his voice and the sound of the drum monkeys rushed up from every direction. It was as packed as the crowds of Parisians on the road to St Cloud at festival time. They kept a respectable distance but when Toango spoke a few kind words and invited them, I believe, to dinner, they came round us one by one.

On the advice of the priest we made as if not to look at them and they took turns to amuse their constitutional monarch. Some carried off rice under their armpits or in their mouths;

others came to steal the crude implements we had brought for them. There are no words and no brushes to describe or paint the movements or facial expressions, the fine and witty demeanour, of those good folk. But what made me both laugh and ponder was the sight of the old wounded monkeys who, leaning on walking sticks, crawled along like our walking wounded on the Quai Bourbon. It needed only a few wooden legs or arms in a sling to present a neat summary of the human condition. Two poor cripples came up as far as the basin of rice giving one another their arms. It was a humbling sight for man – the disguise would have seemed to you, as to me, just too perfect.

When the monkeys had stolen everything they made funny faces for our money, just like the conscientious performers they were, and some did somersaults as children do for alms along the roadside; while others imitated us with gravity and laughed as we do. All these characters were about two-and-a-half feet high. Like children who want to be noticed, they were competing for our attention and outdid each other in trying to interest us with the naughtiness of schoolchildren. Tripping one another up, head-butting an old monkey on the leg or a young one in the back standing to get a view of us – I could go on forever if I had to describe it all.

In the course of my travels I have no doubt seen more interesting things but nothing as amusing as these monkeys in the wild. They recognised their boss because when he passed among them they gathered to caress him. He spoke amicably to the old monkeys who, I swear, seemed to listen to him most attentively.

When we left, these pretty creatures accompanied us back politely. At the border of their equivalent of Pantin or

Montrouge,[9] Toango gave them a few small glasses of liquor which they drank with unbelievable expressions of delight. They screamed with pleasure, jumped head-over-heels, flew through the trees and disappeared half-drunk.

Later on I got to know the priest of the crocodiles and had the perilous honour of seeing these horrible creatures. I know nothing more hateful than their bloodshot eyes or more frightening than their gaping jaws. There are vague similarities between the stupid cruelty of their faces and that of revolutionaries; their overlapping carapaces, their dirty yellow bellies are the very image of insurrectional clothing – they lacked only the red bonnet to make them a symbol of 1793.

We stayed at the edge of a lake where these fearful tyrants lived peacefully. Their priest called them by their names, using some flattering epithets. We had brought turkeys, chickens and two buffalo hindquarters as a feast for the swampy inhabitants of the lake and the first to arrive had a name that corresponded to our word for gentleman.

"Come, my prince; come my fine gentleman; come, my sweet, show me your nose."

At this speech by the Malay, the gentleman lifted his head from the water and arrived at the edge of the lake having made the lake-water foam the length of his route to us. He took a buffalo hindquarter and dived back in. I saw four arrive in turn. There had been five of them in this body of water but a month before my visit one of the crocodile priest's favourites, having devoured a child, was condemned to death by three priests, who, after due legal process killed it and made a touching speech to the other four about the duties of crocodiles as regards children.

9 Districts of Paris.

Lady Wallis suggested a visit to the snakes under the auspices of their high priest, but the sight of the crocodiles had quite put me off these excursions.

It would be easy for me to describe Batavia, Bantam, Surabaya but we have so many prints, screens, lithographs and enamels where you can see Chinese houses, not to mention the misleading set décor in our theatres, that it would be pointless repetition. Besides I have always loathed the type of traveller who scrupulously measured the monuments or sites that they had visited. And since we credit other people quite easily with our own tastes, I will assume you will embrace my hates and my loves. A travel book is a chimera in which the imagination must know how to soar on a magic carpet and if the reader's mind is not perceptive enough to make out the country in question, the leaps and bounds of the narration will suit him no better than boots suit fleas.

Besides there isn't a city in Europe that can give a precise idea of what Batavia is like. Parisians, used to their stinking, badly cleaned streets and ugly plastered walls, could never imagine the luxury and elegance of the houses in Java or Calcutta which get a new coat of white stucco every year. This coating gives the appearance of wealth and shows off the lines of the architecture very clearly. There is in the towns a good number of dwellings that would easily pass for palaces in Europe. The Chinese lend particular importance to street life. But all the glories of the country belong to Europeans. Here their moral power is huge. For example, to make their fortune all they need to do is to be on their feet, in good health, to keep their eyes open and know how to count. But against them are the climate, love, the women, pleasure, indolence and the Chinese. The latter are used to the all-devouring atmosphere and banished forever from their own country, grab control of the commerce and practise theft with audacious impunity. Their skill finds approval even among the judiciary.

An example among the thousand ruses used by the Chinese can demonstrate their scientific approach to theft. It is already organised and always at the ready.

Go inside a shop selling precious cloths; bargain, buy some cashmere or a length of tamava … if you turn your back for a moment while the merchant is rolling up your purchase on the counter, wrapping it and tying it with string, the package flies to the back of the shop and is replaced by another containing inferior goods, that an apprentice has been preparing in the corner of the shop to look exactly like the one you were buying. With no explanation for this miraculous metamorphosis, you return to the shop furious at having been duped by the Chinese everybody had warned you about; but his only response is to laugh at you.

Javanese luxury is so great that the rich are obliged, as everywhere else, to give a value to almost anything. On the day of our departure from France we were assailed by a crowd of merchants offering us a thousand trinkets. To get rid of a watchmaker who clung to me just as typhus descends on a country I offered him three hundred francs each for some very small, plain gold watches. I got them all for one thousand écus. These watches were all the rage in Java and I sold the last ones for six thousand francs. When I only had one left I am too ashamed to reveal what I was offered for it by the most beautiful and richest woman on the island. The memory of her propositions brings back the fine life of Asia and my pleasures, my perfume … Everlasting despair! Nevertheless, human memory, by recalling the image of a vanished happiness, plays the role of a faithful friend – it consoles. And it encourages our hopes for the future by reminding us of wishes that have been satisfied.

At difficult points of my life, now, when I want to prepare a great and splendid party for myself, I think back to my ten months in Java. I lie down on my divans covered in Chinese satin and breathe the scented air of my lost and irretrievable palace. I persuade myself that I can hear again the soft footsteps of my bejewelled slaves; the sun of the Indies still lights up the designs on my cashmeres even through the rice paper blinds; my Bengal sparrows fly and sing around me; my long-necked vases filled with shrubs surround me with their sweet perfume; I am living that tale from Arabia, which was once real for me; finally my pale Javanese lady is there, stretched out in the midst of her black hair like a doe on a bed of leaves.

Ah, Sir! To be satiated in voluptuous languor, inhaling the perfumes that arrive freshly vapourised at the nervous papilla of the soul … to do nothing, to think; to be one's own poet; to bury one's virginal reveries at the bottom of one's heart, believe me, this life is, in our incomplete world, the one which most closely resembles that world of adorable perfection known in all countries as *heaven* and as *paradise* in the Catholic, Roman and Apostolic religion.

But alas! Dreaming thus of the past and then waking up to army call-up papers sent by that Great Whore which we call national *Liberté* is a horrible pain which brings us back to the hell of our Parisian civilisation, where there is shame in pleasure and in passion, where the tax office gets its claws into your new coach or even onto a woman's breast! The East Indies is the motherland of voluptuousness … while Paris, they say, is the motherland of thought. The idea is consoling. But would the consolation offered be more complete if one could meet Javanese women in Paris? But alas, there are only half-Javanese women, without that hair; and although Parisiennes think and are witty, an oriental woman is a sublime animal. But if I wanted to tell all the strange things about this country, I would need more than ten such evenings...

Thank you, said I to the traveller, you have shown us Java while sparing us the nautical problems, the freight, the storms and the Javanese woman.

During the seven more days that I was due to spend in Angoulême, Monsieur Grand-B...n, in whom I had discovered a second volume, in living form, of Sinbad-the-Sailor, told me a thousand more terror-filled tales of love and danger all of which made me thirsty for the Ganges. Then he left me most generously with a number of documents connected with the Indies and which I will try to use for their drama, poetry and imagery in order to make those who know not the power of study, say:

"Where does he find the time to travel?"

Or:

"He's crazy, don't believe a word, he lives off illusion, he has no more been to Java than you or me!"

In truth, soon I will be losing no time in taking the stagecoach once again, travelling back to Paris across the fields of Touraine and Poitou that I thought I should never see again. During my first days back in Paris I had a lot of trouble persuading myself that I had not indeed been to Java, so much had that traveller struck my imagination with his tales. I had hardly dared say that I dreamed of Javanese women and that

I inspected the hair of Parisian women to check if all women with luxuriant hair were white.

Finally, if it were possible to have been in Java more truly than I, who had not been, I defy all travellers, ancient and modern, to enjoy themselves as much there as I did, and to know it as well, and as badly, as I. True or false, these fantastic stories implanted in me the whole of Indian poetry. There are nights and days when the spirit of Asia rises up before me, awakes and lives within me. Then comes a play, acted out on an imaginary sheet pinned up I know not where, with the most fantastical of shadow puppets, which I have the honour of recommending to you all.

Afterword

Although it contains much fantasy, Balzac's information is not all invented and there is some truth in the tales of the Commissioner for Ordnance for Angoulême, Grand-Besançon. He certainly boasted about the *upas* tree, as Pierre Janin has showed in his Preface, but Balzac had to have contacted other informants, in particular his friend Auguste Borget, the painter, who was preparing for his round-the-world voyage at this time (1831). It was probably Borget who told Balzac about the book quoted, *The Story of Lord McCartney's Voyage*, and his publisher, Amherst. This book had been translated into French by J. Castera in 1799. If Balzac had looked into the book he would have seen these words on the subject of the *upas* tree as described by Foersh. "But what he says about a tree so poisonous that its emanations can kill people miles away is regarded in the country itself like one of Baron Munchausen's fables." What a shame that was and how Foersh's fiction seems so much more attractive.

Balzac may perhaps have discussed this very subject with Charles Nodier who published in the same month of November 1832, in the same *Revue de Paris*, 'Le Songe d'Or' (Dream of Gold), in which is written: "All five of them fell asleep forever in the poisoned shade of the *upas* tree, whose deadly seeds from the depths of the forests of Java, one breath of your anger has blown here."

But neither Auguste Borget nor Charles Nodier had been to Java. It must therefore have been Grand-Besançon who gave Balzac the most information. It could be interesting to reconstitute as far as possible what precisely the Commissioner said.

The printed text of *Voyage de Paris à Java* is not the one originally given in to A. Pichot, the publisher of the *Revue de Paris*. The latter gentleman, who had been alarmed by a passage in the text, wrote to Balzac on 23 November 1832: "Your absence has forced me into an act of authority which I would not have made without your agreement. I claim no literary authority, but my conscience, stupefied no doubt by prudishness, forced me to suppress two sentences of your description of Javanese women and their prancing around."

Here is the passage that was removed, much longer than the "two sentences" to which Pichot refers. It was discovered by a M. Louvenjoul: *"There, the female genius has developed further than anywhere else on the globe. There, woman has an innate suppleness and the concentric movements of the most graceful reptiles. She can bend, unbend, crouch, roll, unroll, stand up with the skill of a climbing liana or a convolvulus plant. She seizes upon love with all the chemical ardour of two substances of which one can strip the other of its colour and strength. The body of a Javanese woman seems gifted with fluidity and the rapid twists and turns we so admire in wild animals, when they leap up and flee when surprised while sleeping in a leafy wood. These females flow, sparkle, burst and as a calm sea reflects the sky, they reflect their happiness on their faces dewy with the momentary fatigue of their impassioned eyes."*

Although Balzac was travelling for the whole month of November 1832, he probably did remember his text and thanked Pichot for the cuts on 3 December.

This passage belongs just after: *"Well! I found the fulfilment of these crazed dreams in the typical Javanese marriage"* (on page 26). This sentence should be followed by *"There, the female genius..."*.

Grand-Besançon must also have told stories of Javanese and Malay women killing their faithless lovers – they are innumerable.

Eugène Sue[1], in his *Mystères de Paris*, takes up the same theme: *"Everyone has heard tell of these coloured women, who are so to speak, fatal for European man, of these enchanting vampires who, intoxicating their victim with terrible seductions, drain him of the last drop of blood and his last piece of gold, leaving him as their saying goes, with only tears to drink and his heart to chew on."* And Somerset Maugham again used this theme in 1921 in one of his most famous stories (*P&O*).

1 Eugène Sue (1804–1857), French novelist.

Balzac continues with his description of the Bengal sparrow but he must have confused two of Grand-Besançon's pieces of information. The Javanese do indeed love the Bengal (the *Glatik*) – it's a little blue/grey sparrow with a black-and-white head and a red beak, which lives in the paddy fields to which it brings luck and good harvests. One can see at planting time great flocks of these birds bathing in the smallest puddles. This bird has no song but the Javanese are very partial to the song of one bird, the bulbul (a type of nightingale), which they catch and put in cages that are covered with a black veil because the bird sings above all at dusk. Perhaps the Javanese listening to it, motionless, hear: *"the pearly cascade of the piano, the tenderness of strings, the warm sounds of the physharmonica. It is the cantor of real passion."* This extract takes on a particular charm when one reads in the correspondence with the excellent Madame Hanska,[2] the "Dear Eveline" of passages like this: *"A thousand good pigeonneries[3] from the Bengal sparrow to his dovecote."*

Balzac makes an allusion to William of Orange and to the Belgian revolution[4] which might appear to be of little relevance to Java; but, on the contrary, Grand-Besançon would have told him of the repercussions these events had in Java. They took place just after the revolt in the island of Prince Diponogero, which degenerated into a real war, the Java War (1825–30). Lost by the Javanese, the war gave rise to a whole literature and plays that dealt cruelly with the Dutch. One

2 Madame Evelyne Hanska was Balzac's patron.

3 'Pigeon' is French slang for a dupe, a mug.

4 The Dutch were the colonial masters of the East Indies until after the World War II and the Netherlands and Belgium were one country until 1830.

play, written by Sultan Hamengkubuwana V in 1830, is called *Petruk Becomes King*; in it a clown, Petruk, finds himself King by chance and takes as his title "Scourge of the Belgians". The allusion to William of Orange was clear to everyone in Java at this time. This detail of Balzac's story allows us to date Grand Besançon's journey to 1829 and 1830, and when he met Balzac in 1831 his memories would still have been very fresh.

At the beginning of the 19th century in Europe, 'to run *amok*' usually meant a sort of murderous folly, sudden and inexplicable; opium was not generally thought to be the cause of this dreadful impulse. Even so, as early as 1803, Sydney Smith[5] wrote: "We cannot but believe that one day or another, when they are more intoxicated by opium than usual, the Malays will run amok from Cape Comoro to the Caspian." Balzac is one of the first writers to use the expression in a French text (the Robert dictionary states that the first use of the word in French was in 1832 and it does not appear in the Littré dictionary, but it was used in England in the 15th century).

Tree ferns are numerous in Java particularly in the foothills of volcanoes. They form great clumps which unwind as the plant matures; these clumps are the origin of many Javanese decorative motifs, in particular the tree of life.

When Grand-Besançon told Balzac the stories of men dominating and ordering about animals which respond like humans, he could not fail to be charmed since he was a keen

5 Sydney Smith (1771–1845), English writer and clergyman.

admirer of La Fontaine[6] of whose *Fables* he had just published an edition illustrated by Deveria. This was a commercial failure but Balzac, listening to the Commissioner, must have thought of the words of La Fontaine, in his *Discours à Monsieur le Duc de La Rochefoucauld*, which begin the fourteenth Fable of Book Two:

"I have said to myself often, seeing the way
Men act, and how they behave
On a thousand occasions just like animals:
That their king has no fewer faults than his subjects
And that nature has put in every creature
Some grain of a whole that the mind can draw on
I mean mind-bodies, moulded from matter."

It is in this spirit that Balzac took up Grand-Besançon's stories, mixing up many things. In these paragraphs appear the foreign words he used. *Tomogon* must be a poor transliteration of the Javanese *Tumenggung*, a title bestowed on provincial chiefs; and Toango, the father of the monkeys, must be "*Tunku*", which is the equivalent of "Majesty" in Malay, when addressing a foreign king. This is certainly the case since the father of the monkeys is a Malay and we are in Java. From time immemorial there had been hermits on the island who claimed to have power over animals. But the battle described must have another origin. The good Commissioner must have been telling the Ramayana story. The Javanese version of this Indian epic had been acted out over a long period and

6 Jean de La Fontaine (1621–1695), French poet.

one very popular episode tells the story of Bali, king of the monkeys and his rival, Surgiva, whom he had ousted. The latter emerged victorious from the battle thanks to Rama's intervention. Surgiva, in order to thank him, lends him his army of monkeys commanded by a great white ape, Hanuman. The representation of the battle is acrobatic rather than realistic and the performances of the two monkey chiefs are all leaps, perilous bounds and somersaults. *"Tripping one another up, head-butting an old monkey on the leg or a young one in the back standing to get a view of us I could go on forever if I had to describe it all."*

In the following paragraph Balzac goes on by telling the story of the priest of the crocodiles and there is no doubt that he comes here closest to the story told by his informant. If there are no crocodiles left in Java today, there are still many in Sumatra and other local islands and an Indonesian writer, Sobron Aidit, recounted in 1947 in one of his stories, *Crocodiles and their Dukun*, the following adventure: a fisherman from Biliton island (south-east of Sumatra) was seriously wounded in the leg by a crocodile. In such a case tradition dictates that its companions meet and agree to ask a *dukun* (a healer, or magician – Grand-Besançon calls him a "priest") to capture the guilty one. The story says that the *dukun* speaks the crocodiles' language and has a great influence on them. In the story two crocodiles are captured alive and taken to the village where the *dukun* speaks to one of them. *"It is your fault. If you had been good and had not sinned you wouldn't be here."* The *dukun* spoke with great gentleness to the crocodile (Balzac repeats this same information) and as he plunges his knife into the animal's throat, says to it: *"Hush! Keep calm. You are leaving us and promise me you will be well-behaved in the next world and you will sin no more."* Balzac ends his story in the same vein. It is said in Sumatra that when a crocodile has killed a child, the *dukun* goes to the water's edge where the incident occurred, and calls out to the crocodiles until a young reptile appears and he tells the parents: "See, your child has come back." The young beast is captured and given to the parents who raise it like a child, dressing it and adorning it with jewellery. This is still occasionally practised today, half from belief and half for the tourists to whom they will show the clothed animal, for money. As a pseudo-doctor from the neighbourhood says: "We can, today, no longer believe in these customs as I have analysed the blood of crocodiles and it is not human blood."

Balzac concludes his Journey to Java with an allusion to the shadow puppet theatre where, against "an imaginary sheet pinned up I know not where, with the most fantastical of shadow puppets". The shadow puppet theatre is still popular in Java.

Grand-Besançon, even if he was taken in by the *upas* story and – along with many others – by the stories about the sensuality of Javanese woman, was for the most part a respectable source of information. On many points he provided precise information omitted by many travellers: the popularity of the *glatik* which, even if it doesn't bathe in the rose's corolla, does so in the puddles of the paddy fields. The allusions to William of Orange, in 1831, to the tree ferns, and above all to the crocodile priest make us regret he did not take up his pen to write a report that would have been perhaps less seductive, but more factual.

Balzac, nevertheless, quotes La Fontaine's "Two Pigeons" in a letter (22 July 1825) to the Duchess d'Abrantes:

"I was there; this happened to me
You will think you were there yourself."

Travellers must, he says, inform their readers. But he let his imagination loose and transformed the best information into fables. He makes his text out to be the description of a reverie. He did the same thing when he described the town of Issoudun in *La Rabouilleuse* developing the information given by another friend of the Carraud family, Péréme[7], or when he describes Paris, modifying his youthful memories. With these modifications he gives us a wider and deeper understanding of these towns than geographers do and perhaps that's what he wanted to do all along, giving us a better approach to Java; to respond, for example, to the invitation of Theophile Gautier:

"Say, young beauty, where will you go?
To the Pacific Sea? To the Island of Java?"

Jacques Dumarçay

7 Armand Pérémé, French antiquary.

Bibliography

Balzac, H. de, *Correspondence*, texts compiled, classified and annotated by R. Pierrot, Volume II, 1832–1835, Paris, éd. Garnier, 1962.

Balzac, H. de, *Lettres à Madame Hanska*, integral edition by R. Pierrot, Volume I, 1832–1835, Paris, éd. Le Delta, 1967.

Castex, G., *Balzac et Charles Nodier, L'année balzacienne 1962*, p. 197 and 212, Paris, éd. Garnier, 1962.

Citron, P., *Le rêve asiatique de Balzac, L'année balzacienne 1968*, p. 303 and 336, Paris, éd. Garnier, 1968.

Dumont d'Urville, H., *Voyage pittoresque autour du monde*, Paris, 1834–1835.

Labrousse, P., *Indonésien-français – Dictionnaire général*, Paris, éd. Archipel, 1984.

Lombard, D., *Histoires courtes d'Indonésie*, Paris, E.F.E.O., 1968. 'Les crocodiles et leur dukun', p. 33–41.

Macartney, Lord, *Voyage dans l'intérieur de la Chine et en Tartarie fait dans les années 1792, 1793, 1794*, translated from English, with notes by J. Castera, Paris an 7 de la République (1799) – the passage to Java is described in Chapter 1 of Volume II.

Nodier, Ch., *Contes*, Paris, éd. Garnier, 1961. 'Le songe d'or', p. 349–361.

Skeat, W., *Malay Magic*, London, 1900.

Yule, H, et Burnel, A.C., *Hobson Jobson, A Glossary of Colloquial Anglo-Indian Words and Phrases*, London 1969. On the *upas*, p. 952–959.